# Engineering in Our Everyday Lives

## Reagan Miller

🌳 Crabtree Publishing Company

www.crabtreebooks.com

**Author**
Reagan Miller

**Publishing plan research and development:**
Reagan Miller

**Editor**
Crystal Sikkens

**Proofreader**
Shannon Welbourn

**Design**
Samara Parent

**Photo research**
Reagan Miller
Crystal Sikkens

**Production coordinator
and prepress technician**
Samara Parent

**Print coordinator**
Margaret Amy Salter

**Photographs**
Americanspirit/Dreamstime.com: page 9 (right)
Shutterstock: cleanfotos: page 18
Thinkstock: cover (drawing), page 21 (bottom)
Wikimedia Commons: Lokilech: page 12; Daderot: page 13 (top);
   Ilmari Karonen: page 19 (bottom right)
All other images by Shutterstock

**Library and Archives Canada Cataloguing in Publication**

Miller, Reagan, author
     Engineering in our everyday lives / Reagan Miller.

(Engineering close-up)
Includes index.
Issued in print and electronic formats.
ISBN 978-0-7787-0092-0 (bound).--ISBN 978-0-7787-0099-9 (pbk.).--
ISBN 978-1-4271-9403-9 (pdf).--ISBN 978-1-4271-9399-5 (html)

     1. Engineering--Juvenile literature.  I. Title.

TA149.M55 2013          j620          C2013-906284-X
                                      C2013-906285-8

**Library of Congress Cataloging-in-Publication Data**

Miller, Reagan, author.
  Engineering in our everyday lives / Reagan Miller.
       pages cm. --  (Engineering close-up)
  Includes index.
   ISBN 978-0-7787-0092-0 (reinforced library binding) -- ISBN 978-0-7787-
0099-9 (pbk.) -- ISBN 978-1-4271-9403-9 (electronic pdf) -- ISBN (invalid) 978-
1-4271-9399-5 (electronic html)
  1. Engineering--Juvenile literature. 2. Technology--Juvenile literature. 3.
Engineers--Juvenile literature. 4. Engineering--Vocational guidance--
Juvenile literature.  I. Title.

  TA149.M545 2014
  620--dc23
                                      2013043397

# Crabtree Publishing Company

www.crabtreebooks.com          1-800-387-7650

Printed in Canada/032014/MA20140124

**Published in Canada
Crabtree Publishing**
616 Welland Ave.
St. Catharines, Ontario
L2M 5V6

**Published in the United States
Crabtree Publishing**
PMB 59051
350 Fifth Avenue, 59th Floor
New York, New York 10118

**Published in the United Kingdom
Crabtree Publishing**
Maritime House
Basin Road North, Hove
BN41 1WR

**Published in Australia
Crabtree Publishing**
3 Charles Street
Coburg North
VIC 3058

# Contents

# Can you solve this riddle?

Here is a riddle for you to solve! What does a bridge, running shoes, and a roller coaster have in common?

bridge

running shoes

## The answer is...

They all were created using **engineering**! Engineering is using math, science, and creative thinking to **design** many of the things in our world. To design means to make a plan to do or build something. **Engineers** design things that make our lives easier, safer, and more fun!

roller coaster

# What is technology?

The things that are designed by engineers are called **technologies**. Technologies are created to solve a problem or meet a need. A technology can be simple, such as a pencil. A pencil solves a person's need to write down information. Technology can also be **complex**, or made up of many different parts. A computer meets a person's need to find information quickly.

A computer is a complex technology.

# Is it technology?

People design technologies. Things such as trees and rocks are **natural**, or come from nature. Natural things are not technologies because people do not design them.

## What do you think?

*Look at the pictures below. Which pictures show technologies? Which pictures show things that are natural?*

a backpack

a bird's nest

a soccer ball

lightning

7

# Terrific Tools

**Tools** are one kind of technology that engineers design. Tools are objects that people use to make work easier and faster. How hard would it be to dig a hole without using a shovel? How difficult would it be to clean your carpet without using a vacuum?

*A shovel and a vacuum are both tools that make work easier.*

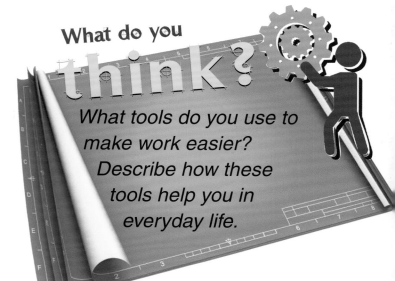

**What do you think?**

*What tools do you use to make work easier? Describe how these tools help you in everyday life.*

## Science tools

Engineers also design tools that help **scientists** discover new things. For example, a **telescope** is a tool that makes far away objects look closer and larger. People can use telescopes to see objects that are too far away to see using only their eyes.

*Telescopes help scientists discover and study objects in space, such as stars and planets.*

9

# Keeping us healthy and safe

Engineers help people by designing technologies that keep us safe and healthy. For example, engineers design tools and machines for doctors to use to help make us well when we are hurt or sick.

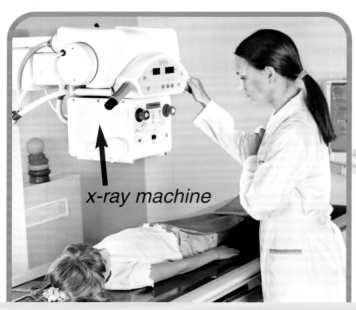

*x-ray machine*

*An **x-ray machine** takes a picture called an **x-ray** that shows the inside of our body.*

*x-ray*

*An x-ray helps doctors learn what is making us sick or if a bone is broken.*

A traffic light is a technology that helps keep our roads safe. How do the other technologies on this page help keep us safe and healthy?

seatbelt

toothbrush and toothpaste

bicycle helmet

sunglasses

11

# Technology is always changing

Engineers design new technologies, but they also look for ways to make the technologies we have better. One example of this is the bicycle. Engineers have changed bicycles over time to make them safer and more fun to ride.

## Ride through history

*In 1816, a man named Baron von Drais designed one of the first bicycles. It had two wooden wheels and no pedals! Riders had to use their feet on the ground to start and stop.*

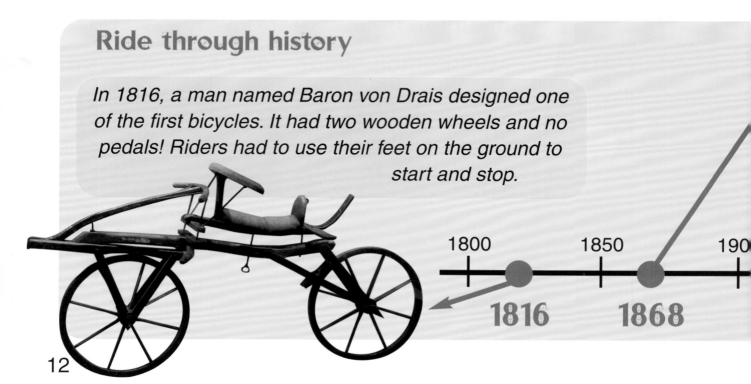

1800      1850      190

**1816**      **1868**

12

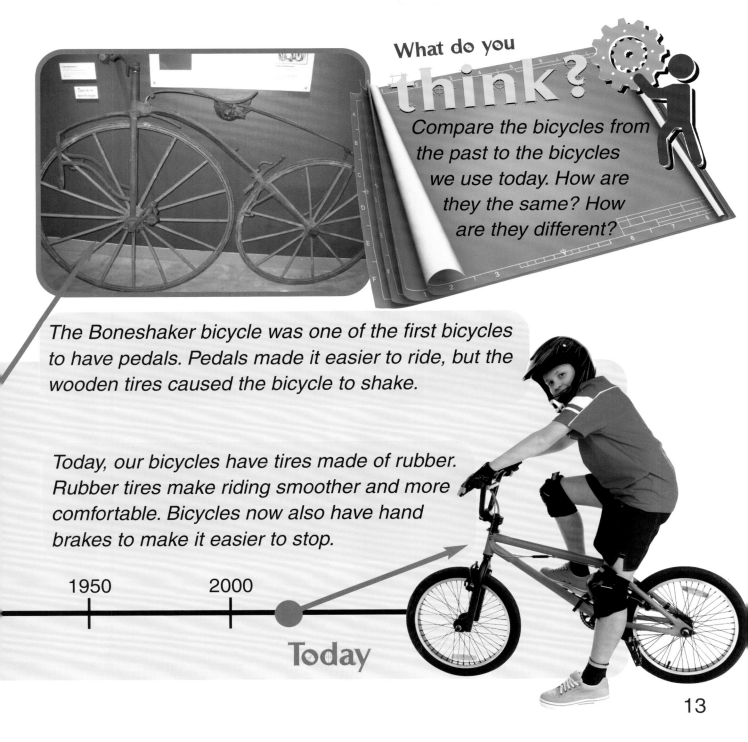

What do you **think?**

Compare the bicycles from the past to the bicycles we use today. How are they the same? How are they different?

The Boneshaker bicycle was one of the first bicycles to have pedals. Pedals made it easier to ride, but the wooden tires caused the bicycle to shake.

Today, our bicycles have tires made of rubber. Rubber tires make riding smoother and more comfortable. Bicycles now also have hand brakes to make it easier to stop.

1950  2000

Today

13

# Think like an engineer!

Engineers believe there is always room for improvement! They are always looking for ways to improve the technologies we use. Engineers improve technologies in different ways, such as making things safer, faster, more comfortable, or easier to use.

The first televisions showed only black and white images. Engineers improved the technology by creating televisions that showed colored images and remote controls to change the channels.

## Your turn!

Think of an object or tool that many people use, such as a bicycle, a cell phone, or a backpack. How could you change the object to make it work better or do something it cannot do now?

**My Improved Bicycle**

**The Rain-or-Shine Rider**

clip-on umbrella

My bicycle is called The Rain-or-Shine Rider. It has an umbrella that clips on the seat. The umbrella keeps me dry when it is raining. It also gives me shade when it is sunny and hot.

*Use the steps below to help you:*
- *Make a list of ideas of how you could improve the object.*
- *Choose your favorite idea. Draw a picture of your object or tool.*
- *Describe the changes you made.*
- *Explain how your changes make the object or tool better and more useful to people.*

# Helpful and harmful

Technologies can be both helpful and harmful. We use technologies everyday to solve problems. Sometimes, however, using a technology can cause problems. For example, a car is a technology that helps people travel quickly from place to place. Cars, however, create **pollution** which is harmful to the **environment**.

*Cars use gasoline to move. Using gasoline creates pollution in the air.*

## Harmful waste

Technology is always changing and improving. But what happens to old technology when new technology is created? Many things get thrown away and end up in **landfills**.

*Technologies such as computers and cell phones are made of materials that do not break down, or slowly disappear. Over time, these items can cause harmful materials to leak into the land around them.*

# Engineers help Earth!

Many engineers work to solve Earth's pollution problems. They design technologies to help make the things we use less harmful to the environment. For example, engineers design electric cars. Electric cars do not use gasoline so they do not create as much pollution.

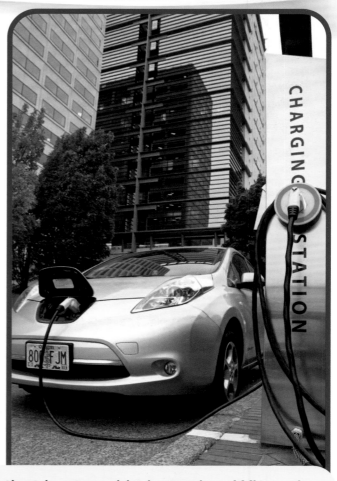

*Many electric cars run on electricity that is stored in batteries. When the electricity runs low, the battery can be recharged at a charging station.*

Engineers designed the surface of this playground to use recycled car tires.

Engineers also help the environment by finding ways to **recycle** things people throw away, such as newspapers and plastic bottles. To recycle means to make something new from something that has been used before.

*Items that can be recycled have this **symbol** on them. Try to buy products that show this symbol.*

19

# Many kinds of engineers

There are many kinds of engineers. Different kinds of engineers work to solve different problems. You can find engineers working in hospitals, offices, forests, and even in space! Read on to learn more about some of the different kinds of engineers and the work they do.

*Environmental engineers* design technologies to help keep the air, soil, and water clean.

**Aerospace engineers** design different kinds of **aircraft**, such as airplanes and space shuttles.

**Civil engineers** design buildings, bridges, tunnels, and roads.

21

# Are you a future engineer?

Engineers help make the world better, safer, and more fun! Do you think you would like to be an engineer? Maybe someday you will design a technology that changes the world!

*If you answer yes to any of these questions, you might be on your way to becoming a future engineer!*

- ☐ Are you creative and like coming up with new ideas?
- ☐ Do you enjoy challenges and solving problems?
- ☐ Do you want to help other people?
- ☐ Do you enjoy taking things apart to figure out how they work?
- ☐ Do you enjoy working with others as part of a team?

# Learning more

## Books

***Engineering the ABC's: How Engineers Shape Our World***
   by Patty O'Brien Novak, Fern Press, 2009.

***Engineering Elephants*** by Emily M. Hunt, Ph.D. and Michelle N.
   Pantoya, Ph.D. AuthorHouse, 2010.

***Rocks, Jeans, and Busy Machines: An Engineering Kids Storybook***
   by Alane Rivera and Raymundo Rivera, Rivera Engineering, 2010.

## Websites

This site has many different engineering design challenges, games, and video links to explore.
pbskids.org/designsquad

This website provides engineering design challenges, interactive games, and up-to-date engineering information.
www.tryengineering.org/

This website offers engineering design challenges and encourages inventive and creative thinking.
www.inventivekids.com

# Words to know

**engineer** (en-juh-NIHR) noun  A person who uses math, science, and creative thinking to design things that solve problems and meet needs

**environment** (en-VY-ruhn-muhnt) noun  All of the living and nonliving things in a place

**landfills** (LAND-fils) noun  Areas of land where waste is buried in earth

**pollution** (puh-LOO-shuhn) noun  Waste that can harm land, water, and air

**recycle** {ree-SAHY-kuhl) verb  To make something new out of something used before

**scientists** (SAHY-uhn-tists) noun  People trained to do research in science to solve problems

**symbol** (SIM-buhl) noun  Letters or a picture used instead of a word or group of words

*A noun is a person, place, or thing. A verb is an action word that tells you what someone or something does.*

# Index